2023
A Year in Bloom
WEEKLY PLANNER
JULY 2022 • DECEMBER 2023

ROCK
POINT

2023 YEAR AT A GLANCE

JANUARY

S	M	T	W	T	F	S
1	2	3	4	5	6	7
8	9	10	11	12	13	14
15	16	17	18	19	20	21
22	23	24	25	26	27	28
29	30	31				

FEBRUARY

S	M	T	W	T	F	S
			1	2	3	4
5	6	7	8	9	10	11
12	13	14	15	16	17	18
19	20	21	22	23	24	25
26	27	28				

MARCH

S	M	T	W	T	F	S
			1	2	3	4
5	6	7	8	9	10	11
12	13	14	15	16	17	18
19	20	21	22	23	24	25
26	27	28	29	30	31	

APRIL

S	M	T	W	T	F	S
						1
2	3	4	5	6	7	8
9	10	11	12	13	14	15
16	17	18	19	20	21	22
23	24	25	26	27	28	29
30						

MAY

S	M	T	W	T	F	S
	1	2	3	4	5	6
7	8	9	10	11	12	13
14	15	16	17	18	19	20
21	22	23	24	25	26	27
28	29	30	31			

JUNE

S	M	T	W	T	F	S
				1	2	3
4	5	6	7	8	9	10
11	12	13	14	15	16	17
18	19	20	21	22	23	24
25	26	27	28	29	30	

JULY

S	M	T	W	T	F	S
						1
2	3	4	5	6	7	8
9	10	11	12	13	14	15
16	17	18	19	20	21	22
23	24	25	26	27	28	29
30	31					

AUGUST

S	M	T	W	T	F	S
		1	2	3	4	5
6	7	8	9	10	11	12
13	14	15	16	17	18	19
20	21	22	23	24	25	26
27	28	29	30	31		

SEPTEMBER

S	M	T	W	T	F	S
					1	2
3	4	5	6	7	8	9
10	11	12	13	14	15	16
17	18	19	20	21	22	23
24	25	26	27	28	29	30

OCTOBER

S	M	T	W	T	F	S
1	2	3	4	5	6	7
8	9	10	11	12	13	14
15	16	17	18	19	20	21
22	23	24	25	26	27	28
29	30	31				

NOVEMBER

S	M	T	W	T	F	S
			1	2	3	4
5	6	7	8	9	10	11
12	13	14	15	16	17	18
19	20	21	22	23	24	25
26	27	28	29	30		

DECEMBER

S	M	T	W	T	F	S
					1	2
3	4	5	6	7	8	9
10	11	12	13	14	15	16
17	18	19	20	21	22	23
24	25	26	27	28	29	30
31						

2024 YEAR AT A GLANCE

JANUARY

S	M	T	W	T	F	S
	1	2	3	4	5	6
7	8	9	10	11	12	13
14	15	16	17	18	19	20
21	22	23	24	25	26	27
28	29	30	31			

FEBRUARY

S	M	T	W	T	F	S
				1	2	3
4	5	6	7	8	9	10
11	12	13	14	15	16	17
18	19	20	21	22	23	24
25	26	27	28	29		

MARCH

S	M	T	W	T	F	S
					1	2
3	4	5	6	7	8	9
10	11	12	13	14	15	16
17	18	19	20	21	22	23
24	25	26	27	28	29	30
31						

APRIL

S	M	T	W	T	F	S
	1	2	3	4	5	6
7	8	9	10	11	12	13
14	15	16	17	18	19	20
21	22	23	24	25	26	27
28	29	30				

MAY

S	M	T	W	T	F	S
			1	2	3	4
5	6	7	8	9	10	11
12	13	14	15	16	17	18
19	20	21	22	23	24	25
26	27	28	29	30	31	

JUNE

S	M	T	W	T	F	S
						1
2	3	4	5	6	7	8
9	10	11	12	13	14	15
16	17	18	19	20	21	22
23	24	25	26	27	28	29
30						

JULY

S	M	T	W	T	F	S
	1	2	3	4	5	6
7	8	9	10	11	12	13
14	15	16	17	18	19	20
21	22	23	24	25	26	27
28	29	30	31			

AUGUST

S	M	T	W	T	F	S
				1	2	3
4	5	6	7	8	9	10
11	12	13	14	15	16	17
18	19	20	21	22	23	24
25	26	27	28	29	30	31

SEPTEMBER

S	M	T	W	T	F	S
1	2	3	4	5	6	7
8	9	10	11	12	13	14
15	16	17	18	19	20	21
22	23	24	25	26	27	28
29	30					

OCTOBER

S	M	T	W	T	F	S
		1	2	3	4	5
6	7	8	9	10	11	12
13	14	15	16	17	18	19
20	21	22	23	24	25	26
27	28	29	30	31		

NOVEMBER

S	M	T	W	T	F	S
					1	2
3	4	5	6	7	8	9
10	11	12	13	14	15	16
17	18	19	20	21	22	23
24	25	26	27	28	29	30

DECEMBER

S	M	T	W	T	F	S
1	2	3	4	5	6	7
8	9	10	11	12	13	14
15	16	17	18	19	20	21
22	23	24	25	26	27	28
29	30	31				

BEGONIA

SYMBOLIC MEANINGS
A fanciful nature; Balance; Be cordial; Beware;
Deformed; Deformity; Fanciful; Fanciful nature;
Forewarn; Goodness; Send a warning.

POSSIBLE POWERS
Heightened awareness; Psychic ability.

"Gardening
makes sense in a
senseless world."
–ANDREW WEIL

JULY 2022

NOTES	SUNDAY	MONDAY	TUESDAY
	3	4	5
		INDEPENDENCE DAY (US)	
	10	11	12
	17	18	19
	24	25	26
	31		

JULY 2022

WEDNESDAY	THURSDAY	FRIDAY	SATURDAY
		1	2
		CANADA DAY (CAN)	
6	7	8	9
13	14	15	16
20	21	22	23
27	28	29	30

BRUGMANSIA
Angel's Trumpet, Maikoa

SYMBOLIC MEANINGS
Fame; Separation.

FOLKLORE AND FACTS
As a large shrub with huge, down-facing,
trumpet-shaped flowers, *Brugmansia* is incredibly
beautiful in full bloom, with a lovely fragrance
both day and night.

June/July

MONDAY (JUNE)	27
TUESDAY (JUNE)	28
WEDNESDAY (JUNE)	29
THURSDAY (JUNE)	30
FRIDAY CANADA DAY (CAN)	1
SATURDAY	2
SUNDAY	3

July 2022

MONDAY INDEPENDENCE DAY (US)

4

TUESDAY

5

WEDNESDAY

6

THURSDAY ◖

7

FRIDAY

8

SATURDAY

9

SUNDAY

10

CITRUS X SINENSIS
Bridal festivities; Brings wisdom;
Chastity; Eternal love; Fruitfulness;
Innocence; Marriage;
Your purity equals your loveliness.

July 2022

MONDAY

11

TUESDAY

12

WEDNESDAY ●

13

THURSDAY

14

FRIDAY 15

SATURDAY 16

SUNDAY 17

COREOPSIS
Always cheerful;
Impatience of happiness;
Impatient of absence; Love at first sight.

July 2022

MONDAY

18

TUESDAY

19

WEDNESDAY ◗

20

THURSDAY

21

FRIDAY   22

SATURDAY   23

SUNDAY   24

AMARANTHUS
Endless love; Fidelity; Immortality;
Never-fading flower; Unwithering.

July 2022

MONDAY

25

TUESDAY

26

WEDNESDAY

27

THURSDAY ○

28

FRIDAY   29

....

SATURDAY   30

....

SUNDAY   31

....

BROWALLIA SPECIOSA
Admiration.

PAPAVER RHOEAS
Common Poppy, Corn Poppy, Corn Rose, Field Poppy, Flanders Poppy, Red Poppy, Red Weed

SYMBOLIC MEANINGS
Avoidance of problems; Consolation; Ephemeral charms; Eternal rest; Eternal sleep; Fun-loving; Good and evil; Imagination; Life and death; Light and darkness; Love; Oblivion; Pleasure; Remembrance.

POSSIBLE POWERS
Ambition; Attitude; Clear thinking; Fertility; Fruitfulness; Harmony; Higher understanding; Invisibility; Logic; Love; Luck; Magic; Manifestation in material form; Money; Sleep; Spiritual concepts; Thought processes.

"I must
have flowers,
always, and
always."
—CLAUDE MONET

AUGUST 2022

NOTES	SUNDAY	MONDAY	TUESDAY
		1	2
		SUMMER BANK HOLIDAY (UK-SCT)	
	7	8	9
	14	15	16
	21	22	23
	28	29	30
		SUMMER BANK HOLIDAY (UK-ENG / NIR / WAL)	

AUGUST 2022

WEDNESDAY	THURSDAY	FRIDAY	SATURDAY
3	4 ◖	5	6
10 ●	11	12	13
17	18 ◗	19	20
24	25	26 ○	27
31			

COSMOS BIPINNATUS
Bidens bipinnata, Bidens Formosa, Bidens lindleyi, Coreopsis Formosa, Cosmea tenuifolia, Cosmos, *Cosmos Formosa, Cosmos hybridus, Cosmos spectabilis, Cosmos tenuifolia, Cosmos tenuifolius,* Garden Cosmos, *Georgia bipinnata,* Mexican Aster

SYMBOLIC MEANINGS
Balance; Beautiful; Come walk with me;
Harmony; Hold my hand and walk with me;
Joy in love and in life; Love flower; Modesty;
Orderly; Ornamental; Peacefulness; Tranquility;
Wholesomeness.

FOLKLORE AND FACTS
Arrange a *Cosmos bipinnatus* bouquet in a home that
needs spiritual harmony restored within it.

August

MONDAY SUMMER BANK HOLIDAY (UK-SCT)

1

TUESDAY

2

WEDNESDAY

3

THURSDAY

4

FRIDAY ☽

5

SATURDAY

6

SUNDAY

7

August 2022

MONDAY

8

TUESDAY

9

WEDNESDAY

10

THURSDAY ●

11

FRIDAY   12

SATURDAY   13

SUNDAY   14

GLADIOLUS
Flower of the gladiators; Generosity;
Integrity; Remembrance;
Strength; Vibrancy.

August 2022

MONDAY

15

TUESDAY

16

WEDNESDAY

17

THURSDAY

18

FRIDAY ◗

19

SATURDAY

20

SUNDAY

21

LATHYRUS ODORATUS
Chastity: Courage:
Friendship: Strength.

August 2022

MONDAY

22

TUESDAY

23

WEDNESDAY

24

THURSDAY

25

FRIDAY   26

SATURDAY ○   27

SUNDAY   28

PHRAGMITES AUSTRALIS
Folly: Indiscretion: Music:
Musical voice: Single blessedness.

PUNICA GRANATUM
Anaar, Apple of Granada, Carthage Apple, Daalim, Garnet Apple, Granatapfel, Grenadier, Malicorio, *Malum granatum*

SYMBOLIC MEANINGS
A first housewarming gift; Abundance; Compassion; Conceit; Conceited; Elegance; Foolishness; Foppery; Fullness; Good luck; Good things; Marriage.

POSSIBLE POWERS
Aphrodisiac; Creative power; Divination; Fertility; Immortality; Intellectual ability; Love; Luck; Passion; Sensuous love; Wealth; Wishes.

FOLKLORE AND FACTS
Carry a piece of *Punica granatum* husk to increase fertility.
• Use a forked branch of *Punica granatum*
as a divining rod to find hidden wealth.

"To nurture
a garden is to feed
not just the body,
but the soul."

–LUTHER BURBANK

SEPTEMBER 2022

NOTES	SUNDAY	MONDAY	TUESDAY
	4	5	6
	FATHER'S DAY (AUS / NZ)	LABOR DAY (US) LABOUR DAY (CAN)	
	11	12	13
	PATRIOT DAY (US) GRANDPARENTS' DAY (US)		
	18	19	20
	○ 25 ROSH HASHANAH (BEGINS AT SUNDOWN)	26	27

SEPTEMBER 2022

WEDNESDAY	THURSDAY	FRIDAY	SATURDAY
	1	2 ◐	3
7	8	9 ●	10
14	15	16 ◑	17
	FIRST DAY OF NATIONAL HISPANIC HERITAGE MONTH		
21	22	23	24
	FALL EQUINOX		
28	29	30	

DAHLIA
Acoctli, Belia, Bishop of Llandaff, Cocoxochitl, Deri, Georgina, Mexican Georgiana, Peony of India, Tenjikubotan

SYMBOLIC MEANINGS
Dignity; Dignity and elegance; Elegance;
Eloquence and dignity; Forever yours; Good taste;
Instability; Novelty; Pomp; Refinement;
Warning of change.

POSSIBLE POWERS
Portent of betrayal; Spiritual evolution.

August/September

MONDAY (AUGUST) SUMMER BANK HOLIDAY (UK-ENG / NIR / WAL)   29

TUESDAY (AUGUST)   30

WEDNESDAY (AUGUST)   31

THURSDAY SUMMER BANK HOLIDAY (UK-SCT)   1

FRIDAY   2

SATURDAY (3

SUNDAY FATHER'S DAY (AUS / NZ)   4

September 2022

MONDAY LABOR DAY (US) / LABOUR DAY (CAN)

5

TUESDAY

6

WEDNESDAY

7

THURSDAY

8

FRIDAY   9

SATURDAY ●   10

SUNDAY PATRIOT DAY (US) / GRANDPARENTS' DAY (US)   11

DIANTHUS BARBATUS
Flower of the gladiators; Generosity;
Integrity; Remembrance;
Strength; Vibrancy.

September 2022

MONDAY

12

TUESDAY

13

WEDNESDAY

14

THURSDAY NATIONAL HISPANIC HERITAGE MONTH BEGINS

15

FRIDAY   16

SATURDAY ◗   17

SUNDAY   18

CALYSTEGIA SEPIUM
Dead hope: Extinguished hopes;
Insinuation.

September 2022

MONDAY

19

TUESDAY

20

WEDNESDAY

21

THURSDAY FALL EQUINOX

22

FRIDAY   23

SATURDAY   24

SUNDAY   ROSH HASHANAH (BEGINS AT SUNDOWN)   25

PORTULACA GRANDIFLORA
Superior merit; Voluptuous love;
Voluptuousness.

TAGETES
Adenopappus, African Marigold, African Marygold, American Marigold, Common Marigold, Diglossus, Drunkards, Enaleida, Herb of the Sun, Marigold, Mary's Gold, Solenotheca, Vilobia

SYMBOLIC MEANINGS
Creativity; Grief; Jealousy; Pain; Passion; Vulgar-minded; Vulgar minds.

POSSIBLE POWERS
Legal matters; Love charms; Prophetic dreams; Protection; Psychic powers.

FOLKLORE AND FACTS
Early Christians would offer *Tagetes* blossoms around statues of the Virgin Mary, in place of coins. • The Welsh believed that *Tagetes* could be used to predict the stormy weather if the flowers did not open in the morning.

"The earth laughs
in flowers."

–RALPH WALDO
EMERSON

OCTOBER 2022

NOTES	SUNDAY	MONDAY	TUESDAY
	◑ 2	3	4
		LABOUR DAY (AUS-ACT / NSW / SA)	YOM KIPPUR (BEGINS AT SUNDOWN)
	● 9	10	11
	SUKKOT (BEGINS AT SUNDOWN)	INDIGENOUS PEOPLES' DAY (US) COLUMBUS DAY (US) THANKSGIVING DAY (CAN)	
	16	◐ 17	18
		SIMCHAT TORAH (BEGINS AT SUNDOWN)	
	23	24 ○	25
		LABOUR DAY (NZ)	
	30	31	
		HALLOWEEN	

OCTOBER 2022

WEDNESDAY	THURSDAY	FRIDAY	SATURDAY
			1
5	6	7	8
12	13	14	15
19	20	21	22
26	27	28	29

ALYSSUM
Alison, *Aurinia saxatilis, Lobularia maritima,*
Sweet Alyssum

SYMBOLIC MEANINGS
Worth beyond beauty.

POSSIBLE POWERS
Calm anger; Moderating anger; Protection.

FOLKLORE AND FACTS
Alyssum will expel negative charms if worn as an amulet.
• *Alyssum* can calm an angry person if it is placed
in their hand or on their body. • When *Alyssum* is hung
in the house it supposedly can protect those in it against
magically imposed illusions and fascinations.

September/October

MONDAY (SEPTEMBER)   26

TUESDAY (SEPTEMBER)   27

WEDNESDAY (SEPTEMBER)   28

THURSDAY (SEPTEMBER)   29

FRIDAY (SEPTEMBER)   30

SATURDAY   1

SUNDAY ☽   2

October 2022

MONDAY LABOUR DAY (AUS-ACT / NSW / SA)

3

TUESDAY YOM KIPPUR (BEGINS AT SUNDOWN)

4

WEDNESDAY

5

THURSDAY

6

FRIDAY

7

SATURDAY

8

SUNDAY SUKKOT (BEGINS AT SUNDOWN) ●

9

CALENDULA OFFICINALIS
Amorousness; Dream magic;
Evil thoughts; Helps with seeing fairies;
Legal matters; Prediction;
Prophetic dreams; Protection;
Psychic powers; Rebirth; Sleep.

October 2022

MONDAY INDIGENOUS PEOPLES' DAY (US) / COLUMBUS DAY (US) / THANKSGIVING DAY (CAN)

10

TUESDAY

11

WEDNESDAY

12

THURSDAY

13

FRIDAY   **14**

· ·

SATURDAY   **15**

· ·

SUNDAY   **16**

· ·

SCABIOSA ATROPURPUREA
Grief, Mourning, Sorrow.

October 2022

MONDAY SIMCHAT TORAH (BEGINS AT SUNDOWN) ◗

17

TUESDAY

18

WEDNESDAY

19

THURSDAY

20

FRIDAY

21

SATURDAY

22

SUNDAY

23

STYLOPHORUM DIPHYLLUM
Joys to come.

October 2022

MONDAY LABOUR DAY (NZ)

24

TUESDAY ○

25

WEDNESDAY

26

THURSDAY

27

FRIDAY

28

SATURDAY

29

SUNDAY

30

CHEIRANTHUS CHEIRI
Bonds of affection;
Enduring beauty;
Everlasting love.

CHRYSANTHEMUM
Chrysanth, Flower of Happiness, Flower of Life,
Flower of the East, Mums

SYMBOLIC MEANINGS
A heart left to desolation; Abundance; Cheerfulness;
Fidelity; Happiness; Loveliness; Optimism; Promotes
mental health; Wealth; You're a wonderful friend.

COLOR MEANING
Rose: In love.
White: Truth.
Yellow: Imperial.

POSSIBLE POWERS
Protection.

FOLKLORE
Chinese Feng Shui suggests that *Chrysanthemum* will
bring happiness into the home.

"You can cut all
the flowers
but you cannot
keep spring
from coming."
—PABLO NERUDA

NOVEMBER 2022

NOTES	SUNDAY	MONDAY	TUESDAY
			◖ 1
			ALL SAINTS' DAY
	6	7	● 8
	DAYLIGHT SAVING TIME ENDS (US / CAN)		ELECTION DAY (US)
	13	14	15
	20	21	22
	27	28	29

NOVEMBER 2022

WEDNESDAY	THURSDAY	FRIDAY	SATURDAY
2	3	4	5
9	10	11 VETERANS DAY (US)	12
◗ 16	17	18	19
○ 23	24 THANKSGIVING DAY (US)	25 NATIVE AMERICAN HERITAGE DAY (US)	26
◖ 30			

ANACAMPTIS PAPILIONACEA
Butterfly Orchid. Pink Butterfly Orchid

SYMBOLIC MEANINGS
Domestic quiet: Gaiety.

FOLKLORE AND FACTS
Anacamptis papilionacea is a ground
orchid that can often be found growing
in hay meadows.

October/November

MONDAY (OCTOBER) HALLOWEEN

31

TUESDAY ALL SAINTS' DAY

1

WEDNESDAY

2

THURSDAY

3

FRIDAY

4

SATURDAY

5

SUNDAY DAYLIGHT SAVING TIME ENDS (US / CAN)

6

November 2022

MONDAY   7

TUESDAY ELECTION DAY (US) ●   8

WEDNESDAY   9

THURSDAY   10

FRIDAY VETERANS DAY (US)

11

SATURDAY

12

SUNDAY

13

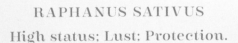

RAPHANUS SATIVUS
High status; Lust; Protection.

November 2022

MONDAY

14

TUESDAY

15

WEDNESDAY ☽

16

THURSDAY

17

FRIDAY   18

SATURDAY   19

SUNDAY   20

SAINTPAULIA
Protection: Spirituality:
Such worth is rare.

November 2022

21

TUESDAY

22

WEDNESDAY ○

23

THURSDAY THANKSGIVING DAY (US)

24

FRIDAY   25

SATURDAY   26

SUNDAY   27

SMILAX
Loveliness: Lovely: Mythology.

NARCISSUS
**Daffadown Dilly, Daffodil, Daffydowndilly, Great Daffodil,
*Narcissus major***

SYMBOLIC MEANINGS
Annunciation; Appreciation of honesty; Beauty; Chivalry;
Clarity of thought; Contentment; Deceitful hopes; Egotism;
Energy that comes from being in love; Excessive self-love;
Faith; Forgiveness; Formality; Forthrightness; High regards.

POSSIBLE POWERS
Aphrodisiac; Fertility; Love; Luck.

FOLKLORE AND FACTS
The *Narcissus* is the flower of the Underworld. •
Wear a *Narcissus* flower over your heart for good luck.
• During medieval times in Europe it was thought that if a
Narcissus drooped while it was being looked at, it was an
omen of death. • The Chinese believe that the *Narcissus* is
lucky and will bring good luck for an entire year if forced
to bloom during the Chinese New Year.

"Minds are
like flowers;
they open only
when the time
is right."

–STEPHEN RICHARDS

DECEMBER 2022

NOTES	SUNDAY	MONDAY	TUESDAY
	4	5	6
	11	12	13
	18	19	20
	HANUKKAH (BEGINS AT SUNDOWN)		
	25 CHRISTMAS DAY	26 BOXING DAY (UK / CAN / AUS / NZ) KWANZAA	27

DECEMBER 2022

WEDNESDAY	THURSDAY	FRIDAY	SATURDAY
	1 WORLD AIDS DAY	2	3 INTERNATIONAL DAY OF PERSONS WITH DISABILITIES
● 7	8	9	10 HUMAN RIGHTS DAY
14	15	☽ 16 6-3 PNH 3-7 Janets	17 TEDS
21 6-3 PNH WINTER SOLSTICE	22 6-3 PNH	○ 23	24 CHRISTMAS EVE
28	☾ 29	30	31 NEW YEAR'S EVE

VIOLA
Heartsease, Pansy, Violet

SYMBOLIC MEANINGS

Affection; Artistic ability; Faithfulness; Fidelity; Honesty;
Loyalty; Modesty; Simplicity; Think of me; Thoughts;
Thoughtful recollection; Virtue.

POSSIBLE POWERS

Calms tempers; Divination; Induces
sleep; Love; Psychic sensitivity.

November/December

MONDAY (NOVEMBER) — 28

TUESDAY (NOVEMBER) — 29

WEDNESDAY (NOVEMBER) ◖ — 30

THURSDAY WORLD AIDS DAY — 1

FRIDAY — 2

SATURDAY INTERNATIONAL DAY OF PERSONS WITH DISABILITIES — 3

SUNDAY — 4

December 2022

MONDAY

5

TUESDAY

6

WEDNESDAY ●

7

THURSDAY

8

FRIDAY	9

SATURDAY HUMAN RIGHTS DAY	10

SUNDAY	11

GUARIANTHE SKINNERI
Mature charm; Prudence;
Sophistication.

December 2022

MONDAY

12

TUESDAY

13

WEDNESDAY

14

THURSDAY

15

FRIDAY ◗   16

SATURDAY   17

SUNDAY HANUKKAH (BEGINS AT SUNDOWN)   18

PELARGONIUM ZONALE
Fertility; Health; Love; Protection.

December 2022

MONDAY

19

TUESDAY

20

WEDNESDAY WINTER SOLSTICE

21

THURSDAY

22

FRIDAY ○   23

SATURDAY CHRISTMAS EVE   24

SUNDAY CHRISTMAS DAY   25

SORBUS
Balance; Connection; Mystery;
Transformation.

GALANTHUS NIVALIS
Candlemas Bells, Church Flower, Common Snowdrop, Dingle-Dangle, Fair Maid of February, February Fairmaids, Maids of February, Mary's Tapers, Perce-Neige, Snowdrop, Snow Piercers

SYMBOLIC MEANINGS
Consolation; Friend in adversity; Friend in need; Hope; Hope in sorrow; Purity and hope.

FOLKLORE AND FACTS
There is a superstition that it is unlucky to bring *Galanthus nivalis* into the home, and that supposedly merely the sight of a single *Galanthus nivalis* growing in the garden foretold a pending disaster.

"In search of my
mother's garden,
I found my own."
–ALICE WALKER

JANUARY 2023

NOTES	SUNDAY	MONDAY	TUESDAY
	1 NEW YEAR'S DAY	2 BANK HOLIDAY (UK-SCT)	3
	8	9	10
	15	16 CIVIL RIGHTS DAY MARTIN LUTHER KING JR. DAY (US)	17
	22 CHINESE NEW YEAR	23	24
	29	30	31

JANUARY 2023

WEDNESDAY	THURSDAY	FRIDAY	SATURDAY
4	5 ●	6	7
11	12	13 ☽	14
18	19	20 ○	21
25	26 AUSTRALIA DAY	27 ☾ HOLOCAUST REMEMBRANCE DAY	28

DIANTHUS CARYOPHYLLUS

SYMBOLIC MEANINGS
Admiration; Bad luck; Bonds of affection; Dignity;
Disappointed; Disdain; Distinction; Fascination; Good
fortune; Good luck; Gratitude; Health and energy.

SPECIFIC COLOR MEANINGS
Pink: A mother's love; A mother's undying love; A woman's
love; Always on my mind; Deep love; I'll never forget you;
Mother's Day symbol; Sentimental love; Woman's love.
Red: Admiration; Affection; Ardent love; Deep romantic
love; Desire; Forlorn; Pure and ardent love.

POSSIBLE POWERS
Divination; Healing; Luck; Protection; Strength.

FOLKLORE AND FACTS
A corsage or nosegay made up of a *Dianthus caryophyllus*,
a sprig of *Rosmarinus officinalis*, and a Geranium flower
means: Love, Fidelity, and Hope. • Fresh red *Dianthus
caryophyllus* in the room of a convalescing patient will
promote strength and energy.

December/January

MONDAY (DECEMBER) BOXING DAY (UK / CAN / AUS / NZ) / KWANZAA   26

TUESDAY (DECEMBER)   27

WEDNESDAY (DECEMBER)   28

THURSDAY (DECEMBER) ◖   29

FRIDAY (DECEMBER)   30

SATURDAY (DECEMBER) NEW YEAR'S EVE   31

SUNDAY NEW YEAR'S DAY   1

January 2023

MONDAY BANK HOLIDAY (UK-SCT)

2

TUESDAY

3

WEDNESDAY

4

THURSDAY

5

FRIDAY ● 6

SATURDAY 7

SUNDAY 8

SUTHERLANDIA FRUTESCENS
Bitter: Dispel darkness:
Spear of the blood.

January 2023

MONDAY

9

TUESDAY

10

WEDNESDAY

11

THURSDAY

12

FRIDAY   **13**

SATURDAY ☽   **14**

SUNDAY   **15**

ROSA X DAMASCENA
Bashful love; Brilliant complexion;
Freshness; Inspiration for love;
Refreshing love.

January 2023

MONDAY CIVIL RIGHTS DAY / MARTIN LUTHER KING JR. DAY (US)

16

TUESDAY

17

WEDNESDAY

18

THURSDAY

19

FRIDAY   20

SATURDAY ○   21

SUNDAY CHINESE NEW YEAR   22

DODECATHEON

Divine beauty; Divinity; My divinity;
Native grace; Pensiveness; Rusticity;
Treasure finding; Winning grace;
You are my divinity; Youthful beauty.

January 2023

MONDAY

23

TUESDAY

24

WEDNESDAY

25

THURSDAY AUSTRALIA DAY

26

FRIDAY HOLOCAUST REMEMBRANCE DAY

27

SATURDAY ◖

28

SUNDAY

29

LILIUM SUPERBUM
Chivalry; Knight; Misanthropy;
Pride; Wealth.

HESPERIS MATRONALIS
**Damask Violet, Dame's Gilliflower, Dame's
Rocket, Dame's Violet, Dames-Wort, Julienne
des Dames, Mother-of-the-Evening, Night-scented
Gilliflower, Queen's Gilliflower, Queen's Rocket,
Rogue's Gilliflower, Summer Lilac, Sweet Rocket,
Winter Gilliflower**

SYMBOLIC MEANINGS
**Fashion; Fashionable;Watchfulness; You are the queen
of coquettes.**

SPECIFIC COLOR MEANING
White: Despair not; God is everywhere.

"The rose is
the flower and
handmaiden
of love—the lily,
her fair associate,
is the emblem of
beauty and purity."
–DOROTHEA DIX

FEBRUARY 2023

NOTES	SUNDAY	MONDAY	TUESDAY
	● 5	6	7
	WAITANGI DAY (NZ)	WAITANGI DAY OBSERVED (NZ)	
	12	◐ 13	14
			VALENTINE'S DAY
	19	○ 20	21
		PRESIDENTS' DAY (US)	
	26	◑ 27	28

FEBRUARY 2023

WEDNESDAY	THURSDAY	FRIDAY	SATURDAY
1 FIRST DAY OF BLACK HISTORY MONTH	2 GROUNDHOG DAY (US / CAN)	3	4
8	9	10	11
15	16	17	18
22 ASH WEDNESDAY	23	24	25

IRIS GERMANICA

SYMBOLIC MEANINGS
Flame.

POSSIBLE POWERS
Divination; Love; Protection; Purification; Root (Orris Root); Wisdom.

FOLKLORE AND FACTS
In Japan the *Iris germanica* root was considered protection against evil spirits and would be hung from the eaves in homes. • An interesting and unusual divination pendulum can be created using a whole *Iris germanica* root suspended by a cord from an *Ipomoea batatas* tuber (yam).

January/February

MONDAY (JANUARY)

30

TUESDAY (JANUARY)

31

WEDNESDAY FIRST DAY OF BLACK HISTORY MONTH

1

THURSDAY GROUNDHOG DAY (US / CAN)

2

FRIDAY

3

SATURDAY

4

SUNDAY WAITANGI DAY (NZ) ●

5

February 2023

MONDAY WAITANGI DAY OBSERVED (NZ)

6

TUESDAY

7

WEDNESDAY

8

THURSDAY

9

FRIDAY   **10**

. . . .

SATURDAY   **11**

. . . .

SUNDAY   **12**

. . . .

LIRIODENDRON
Fame; Rural happiness.

February 2023

MONDAY ☽

13

TUESDAY VALENTINE'S DAY

14

WEDNESDAY

15

THURSDAY

16

FRIDAY 17

SATURDAY 18

SUNDAY 19

TULIPA

A declaration of love; A lover's heart darkened
by the heart of passion; Absolute romance;
Adjustment; Advancement; Aspiration;
Charity; Declaration of love; Determination;
Dreaminess; Elegance and grace.

February 2023

MONDAY PRESIDENTS' DAY (US) ○

20

TUESDAY

21

WEDNESDAY ASH WEDNESDAY

22

THURSDAY

23

FRIDAY   24

SATURDAY   25

SUNDAY   26

NELUMBO NUCIFERA
Beauty; Chastity; Divine female
fertility; Eloquence; Estranged
love; Evolution; Potential; Purity;
Resurrection; Spiritual promises;
Truth; Virtuous.

TROPAEOLUM
Indian Cress, Nasties, Nasturtium

SYMBOLIC MEANINGS
Charity; Conquest; Maternal love; Paternal love; Patriotism;
Resignation; Splendor; Victory in battle; Warlike trophy.

POSSIBLE POWERS
Knowledge; Protection; Psychic sight; Reincarnation;
Study; Uncrossing.

"Happiness held
is the seed;
Happiness shared
is the flower."

–JOHN HARRIGAN

MARCH 2023

NOTES	SUNDAY	MONDAY	TUESDAY
	5	6 ●	7
		PURIM (BEGINS AT SUNDOWN)	
	12	13	14
	DAYLIGHT SAVING TIME BEGINS (US / CAN)	LABOUR DAY (AUS-VIC)	
	19	20 ○	21
	MOTHERING SUNDAY (UK)	SPRING EQUINOX	NOWRUZ
	26	27 ◐	28

MARCH 2023

WEDNESDAY	THURSDAY	FRIDAY	SATURDAY
1 FIRST DAY OF WOMEN'S HISTORY MONTH	2	3	4
8	9	10	11
15	16	17 ST. PATRICK'S DAY	18
22 RAMADAN (BEGINS AT SUNDOWN)	23	24	25
29	30	31	

KALANCHOE
Kalan Chau, Kalanchauhuy, Kalanchoe, Kalanchöe

SYMBOLIC MEANINGS
Endurance; Eternal love; Lasting
affection; Persistence; Your temper
is too hasty.

FOLKLORE AND FACTS
All flowering *Kalanchoe* plants will
bloom for eight weeks.

February/March

MONDAY (FEBRUARY) ◖   **27**

TUESDAY (FEBRUARY)   **28**

WEDNESDAY FIRST DAY OF WOMEN'S HISTORY MONTH   **1**

THURSDAY   **2**

FRIDAY   **3**

SATURDAY   **4**

SUNDAY   **5**

March 2023

MONDAY PURIM (BEGINS AT SUNDOWN)

6

TUESDAY ●

7

WEDNESDAY

8

THURSDAY

9

FRIDAY   **10**

SATURDAY   **11**

SUNDAY DAYLIGHT SAVING TIME BEGINS (US / CAN)   **12**

PHILADELPHUS
Counterfeit; Deceit; Fraternal regard;
Memory; Uncertainty.

March 2023

MONDAY LABOUR DAY (AUS-VIC)

13

TUESDAY

14

WEDNESDAY)

15

THURSDAY

16

FRIDAY ST. PATRICK'S DAY

17

SATURDAY

18

SUNDAY MOTHERING SUNDAY (UK)

19

VIOLA TRICOLOR

Caring; Cheerfulness; Fond memories
of the love and kindness of those who
have passed; Forget-me-not; Memory;
Merriment; Reflection; Remembrance.

March 2023

MONDAY SPRING EQUINOX

20

TUESDAY NOWRUZ ○

21

WEDNESDAY RAMADAN (BEGINS AT SUNDOWN)

22

THURSDAY

23

FRIDAY

24

SATURDAY

25

SUNDAY

26

LYCORIS RADIATA
Abandonment: Flower of the
Afterlife: Hopeful but tragic
fate of lovers: Lost memory:
Never to meet again.

BELLIS PERENNIS
Aster bellis, Baimwort, *Bellis alpina*, *Bellis armena*, *Bellis croatica*, *Bellis hortensis*, *Bellis hybrida*, Common Daisy, English Daisy, Garden Daisy, Lawn Daisy

SYMBOLIC MEANINGS
Beauty; Beauty and innocence; Cheer; Childlike playfulness; Creativity; Decisions; Faith; Gentleness; Purity; Simplicity.

POSSIBLE POWERS
Divination; Divination for love; Heightened awareness; Inner strength; Love; Lust.

FOLKLORE AND FACTS
It was once believed that if a *Bellis perennis* chain were wrapped around a child, the flower chain would protect the child from being stolen by fairies • It was once believed that whoever it is that picks the very first *Bellis perennis* flower of the season will be uncontrollably flirtatious.

"Flowers are
the music
of the ground.
From earth's
lips spoken
without sound."
–EDWIN CURRAN

APRIL 2023

NOTES	SUNDAY	MONDAY	TUESDAY
	2	3	4
	PALM SUNDAY		
	9	10	11
	EASTER		
	16	17	18
	ORTHODOX EASTER	YOM HASHOAH (BEGINS AT SUNDOWN)	
	23	24	25
	30		ANZAC DAY (AUS / NZ)

APRIL 2023

WEDNESDAY	THURSDAY	FRIDAY	SATURDAY
			1 APRIL FOOLS' DAY
5 ● PASSOVER (BEGINS AT SUNDOWN)	6	7 GOOD FRIDAY	8
12 ◐	13	14	15
19 ○	20	21 EID AL-FITR (BEGINS AT SUNDOWN)	22 EARTH DAY
26 ◐ ADMINISTRATIVE PROFESSIONALS' DAY (US)	27	28	29

LATHYRUS ODORATUS
Sweet Pea

SYMBOLIC MEANINGS
A meeting; Blissful pleasure; Chastity;
Delicacy; Departure; Goodbye; I think of
you; Meeting; Thank you for a lovely time.

POSSIBLE POWERS
Chastity; Courage; Friendship; Strength.

FOLKLORE AND FACTS
Wear *Lathyrus odoratus* for strength. •
To keep someone chaste, place a nosegay of *Lathyrus
odoratus* flowers in a vase in their bedroom. •
Fresh *Lathyrus odoratus* flowers forge friendships. •
Hold a *Lathyrus odoratus* flower in your hand to
encourage the truth to be told to you.

March/April

MONDAY (MARCH) — **27**

TUESDAY (MARCH) SUMMER BANK HOLIDAY (UK-SCT) ◗ — **28**

WEDNESDAY (MARCH) — **29**

THURSDAY (MARCH) — **30**

FRIDAY (MARCH) — **31**

SATURDAY APRIL FOOLS' DAY — **1**

SUNDAY PALM SUNDAY — **2**

April 2023

MONDAY

3

TUESDAY

4

WEDNESDAY PASSOVER (BEGINS AT SUNDOWN)

5

THURSDAY ●

6

FRIDAY GOOD FRIDAY

7

SATURDAY

8

SUNDAY EASTER

9

AQUILEGIA
Courage; Cuckoldry; Deserted Love;
Desertion; Folly; Foolishness; Love;
Strength; Wisdom.

April 2023

MONDAY

10

TUESDAY

11

WEDNESDAY

12

THURSDAY ☽

13

FRIDAY   **14**

SATURDAY   **15**

SUNDAY ORTHODOX EASTER   **16**

LAVANDULA ANGUSTIFOLIA

Constancy; Devotion; Distrust; Faith;
Faithful; Humility; Love.

April 2023

MONDAY YOM HASHOAH (BEGINS AT SUNDOWN)　17

TUESDAY　18

WEDNESDAY　19

THURSDAY ○　20

FRIDAY EID AL-FITR (BEGINS AT SUNDOWN)

21

SATURDAY EARTH DAY

22

SUNDAY

23

CACTACEAE
Ardent love; Bravery; Burns with Love;
Chastity; Endurance; Lust; Maternal love;
Protection; Sex; Warmth.

April 2023

MONDAY

24

TUESDAY ANZAC DAY (AUS / NZ)

25

WEDNESDAY ADMINISTRATIVE PROFESSIONALS' DAY (US)

26

THURSDAY ◖

27

FRIDAY   28

SATURDAY   29

SUNDAY   30

ALLIUM SCHOENOPRASUM
Healing: Promotes psychic powers:
Protection from evil:
Protection from negativity.

CONVALLARIA MAJALIS
Convall Lily, Convallaria, Jacob's Ladder, Jacob's Tears,
Ladder to Heaven, Lily Constancy, Lily of the Valley, May
Bells, May Lily, Muguet, Our Lady's Tears

SYMBOLIC MEANINGS
Christ's second coming; Fortune in love;
Good luck; Happiness and purity of heart; Humility; Joy;
Purity of heart; Return of happiness; Returning happiness;
Sociability; Sweet; Sweetness; Tears of the Virgin Mary

POSSIBLE POWERS
Happiness; Healing; Making the right choice;
Mental clarity; Mental powers; Power of people to visualize
a better world.

FOLKLORE AND FACTS
Put *Convallaria majalis* in a room to uplift and cheer all
the people in it.

"Show me your
garden and
I shall tell you
what you are."
–ALFRED AUSTIN

MAY 2023

NOTES	SUNDAY	MONDAY	TUESDAY
		1 LABOUR DAY (AUS–QLD) EARLY MAY BANK HOLIDAY (UK) FIRST DAY OF ASIAN AMERICAN AND PACIFIC ISLANDER HERITAGE MONTH	**2**
	7	**8**	**9**
	14 MOTHER'S DAY (US / CAN)	**15**	**16**
	21	**22** VICTORIA DAY (CAN)	**23**
	28	**29** SPRING BANK HOLIDAY (UK) MEMORIAL DAY (US)	**30**

MAY 2023

WEDNESDAY	THURSDAY	FRIDAY	SATURDAY
3	4 ●	5	6
		CINCO DE MAYO	
10	11 ☽	12	13
17	18 ○	19	20
24	25	26 ☾	27
31			

CRATAEGUS
Bread and Cheese Tree, *Crataegus monogyna 'Biflora'*,
English Hawthorn, Gaxels, Glastonbury Thorn,
Hagthorn, Halves, Haw, Hawberry Tree

SYMBOLIC MEANINGS
Chastity; Contradictions; Duality; Hope; Male energy;
Spring; Union of opposites.

POSSIBLE POWERS
Chastity; Continuity; Death; Fertility; Fishing magic;
Happiness; Hope.

FOLKLORE AND FACTS
Because of its correspondence with fertility, *Crataegus* has
been added into spring wedding flowers. • Put *Crataegus*
under a mattress and around a bedroom to maintain or
even enforce chastity. • Tuck a *Crataegus* leaf into your
hat to promote a good catch when fishing. • Wear a spring
of *Crataegus* if troubled, sad, or depressed to help return
you to a state of happiness. • Sprigs or leaves of *Crataegus*
placed around the home will protect it against lightning
and storm damage. • *Crataegus* is sacred to fairies.

May

MONDAY LABOUR DAY (AUS-QLD) / EARLY MAY BANK HOLIDAY (UK) /
FIRST DAY OF ASIAN AMERICAN AND PACIFIC ISLANDER HERITAGE MONTH

1

TUESDAY

2

WEDNESDAY

3

THURSDAY

4

FRIDAY CINCO DE MAYO ●

5

SATURDAY

6

SUNDAY

7

May 2023

MONDAY

8

TUESDAY

9

WEDNESDAY

10

THURSDAY

11

FRIDAY)   **12**

SATURDAY   **13**

SUNDAY MOTHER'S DAY (US / CAN)   **14**

LEONTOPODIUM NIVALE
Courage: Daring: Invisibility:
Nobility: Power.

May 2023

MONDAY

15

TUESDAY

16

WEDNESDAY

17

THURSDAY

18

FRIDAY ○ **19**

SATURDAY **20**

SUNDAY **21**

ECHINACEA
Health; Immunity; Shielded;
Spiritual warfare; Strength.

May 2023

MONDAY <small>VICTORIA DAY (CAN)</small>

22

TUESDAY

23

WEDNESDAY

24

THURSDAY

25

FRIDAY

26

SATURDAY ◖

27

SUNDAY

28

ERYNGIUM
Attraction; Independence; Love; Lust;
Peace; Severity; Traveler's luck.

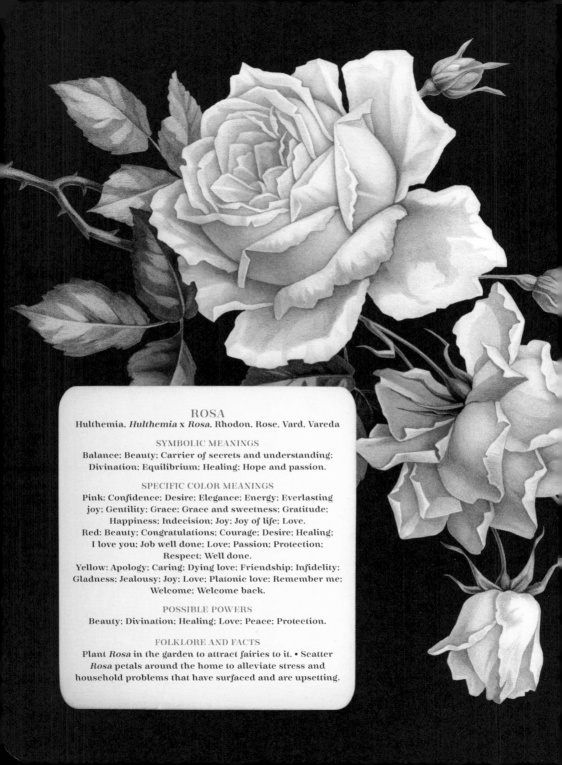

ROSA
Hulthemia, *Hulthemia* x *Rosa*, Rhodon, Rose, Vard, Vareda

SYMBOLIC MEANINGS
Balance; Beauty; Carrier of secrets and understanding;
Divination; Equilibrium; Healing; Hope and passion.

SPECIFIC COLOR MEANINGS
Pink: Confidence; Desire; Elegance; Energy; Everlasting
joy; Gentility; Grace; Grace and sweetness; Gratitude;
Happiness; Indecision; Joy; Joy of life; Love.
Red: Beauty; Congratulations; Courage; Desire; Healing;
I love you; Job well done; Love; Passion; Protection;
Respect; Well done.
Yellow: Apology; Caring; Dying love; Friendship; Infidelity;
Gladness; Jealousy; Joy; Love; Platonic love; Remember me;
Welcome; Welcome back.

POSSIBLE POWERS
Beauty; Divination; Healing; Love; Peace; Protection.

FOLKLORE AND FACTS
Plant *Rosa* in the garden to attract fairies to it. • Scatter
Rosa petals around the home to alleviate stress and
household problems that have surfaced and are upsetting.

"All gardening
is landscape
painting."
–WILLIAM KENT

JUNE 2023

NOTES	SUNDAY	MONDAY	TUESDAY
	4	5	6
	11	12	13
○	18	19	20
	FATHER'S DAY (US / CAN / UK)	JUNETEENTH (US)	
	25 ◖	26	27

JUNE 2023

WEDNESDAY	THURSDAY	FRIDAY	SATURDAY
	1	2	● 3
	FIRST DAY OF PRIDE MONTH		
7	8	9 ☽	10
14	15	16	17
FLAG DAY (US)			
21	22	23	24
SUMMER SOLSTICE			
28	29	30	

LONICERA JAPONICA
Er Hua, Geumeunhwa, Japanese Honeysuckle, Jin Yín Hua,
Ren Dong Téng, Shuang Hua, Suikazura

SYMBOLIC MEANINGS
Affection; Bonds of love; Devoted;
Generous.

POSSIBLE POWERS
Money; Protection; Psychic powers.

May/June

MONDAY (MAY) SPRING BANK HOLIDAY (UK) / MEMORIAL DAY (US) — 29

TUESDAY (MAY) — 30

WEDNESDAY (MAY) — 31

THURSDAY FIRST DAY OF PRIDE MONTH — 1

FRIDAY — 2

SATURDAY ● — 3

SUNDAY — 4

June 2023

MONDAY

5

TUESDAY

6

WEDNESDAY

7

THURSDAY

8

FRIDAY   9

SATURDAY ☽   10

SUNDAY   11

HYBRID TEA
Always lovely; Desire; Enduring desire;
I'll remember, always.

June 2023

TUESDAY

13

WEDNESDAY FLAG DAY (US)

14

THURSDAY

15

FRIDAY

16

. . . .

SATURDAY

17

. . . .

SUNDAY FATHER'S DAY (US / CAN / UK) ○

18

IMPATIENS
Ardent love; Impatience; Impatient
resolves; Touch-Me-Not; Touch
me not; Waiting is difficult for me to do.

June 2023

MONDAY JUNETEENTH HOLIDAY

19

TUESDAY

20

WEDNESDAY SUMMER SOLSTICE

21

THURSDAY

22

FRIDAY

23

SATURDAY

24

SUNDAY

25

FUCHSIA
Amiability; Confiding love;
Faithfulness; Frailty; Frugality; Good
taste; Humble love; Love secrets.

CONSOLIDA
Larkspur

SYMBOLIC MEANINGS
Levity; Lightness; Open heart; Swiftness.

SPECIFIC COLOR MEANING
Pink: Fickleness; Lightness.
Purple: Haughtiness.

POSSIBLE POWERS
Fend off ghosts; Fend off scorpions; Fend off venomous creatures; Health; Protection.

FOLKLORE AND FACTS
Consolida is believed to keep ghosts away.

"The most lasting and pure gladness comes to me from my gardens."

–LILLIE LANGTRY

JULY 2023

NOTES	SUNDAY	MONDAY	TUESDAY
	2 ●	3	4
			INDEPENDENCE DAY (US)
◗	9	10	11
	16 ○	17	18
	23	24 ◖	25
	30	31	

JULY 2023

WEDNESDAY	THURSDAY	FRIDAY	SATURDAY
			1 CANADA DAY (CAN)
5	6	7	8
12	13	14	15
19	20	21	22
26	27	28	29

NYMPHAEA ALBA
European White Waterlily, Nenuphar, White Lotus

SYMBOLIC MEANINGS
Eloquence; Modesty; Persuasion; Purity.

POSSIBLE POWERS
Aphrodisiac; Healing; Peace; Pleasure; Purity; Spiritual enlightenment.

FOLKLORE AND FACTS
Nymphaea alba is believed to be Great Britain's largest flower. • The fragrance of *Nymphaea alba* is believed to have healing power. • *Nymphaea alba* can be used in any spell that is intended to reduce a sexual craving.

June/July

MONDAY (JUNE) ☾   **26**

TUESDAY (JUNE)   **27**

WEDNESDAY (JUNE)   **28**

THURSDAY (JUNE)   **29**

FRIDAY (JUNE)   **30**

SATURDAY CANADA DAY (CAN)   **1**

SUNDAY   **2**

July 2023

MONDAY ● 3

TUESDAY INDEPENDENCE DAY (US) 4

WEDNESDAY 5

THURSDAY 6

FRIDAY

7

SATURDAY

8

SUNDAY ◗

9

CLIVIA MINIATA
Extrovert; Good fortune;
Long life.

July 2023

MONDAY

10

TUESDAY

11

WEDNESDAY

12

THURSDAY

13

FRIDAY 14

SATURDAY 15

SUNDAY 16

DIGITALIS PURPUREA
A wish; Deception; Insincerity;
Mystery; Occupation;
Stateliness; Youth.

July 2023

MONDAY ○   **17**

TUESDAY   **18**

WEDNESDAY   **19**

THURSDAY   **20**

FRIDAY 21

SATURDAY 22

SUNDAY 23

DICTAMNUS ALBUS
Fire; Passion;
Perfected loveliness.

July 2023

MONDAY

24

TUESDAY ◖

25

WEDNESDAY

26

THURSDAY

27

FRIDAY

28

SATURDAY

29

SUNDAY

30

DIONAEA MUSCIPULA
Artifice; Caught at last;
Confinement; Deceit; Incarceration.

RANUNCULUS ACRIS
Meadow Buttercup, *Ranunculus acer, Ranunculus stevenii,*
Tall Buttercup, Tall Field Buttercup

SYMBOLIC MEANINGS
Ambition; Childhood reminiscence; Childishness;
Ingratitude; Memories of childhood; Perfidy; Riches; Self-
esteem; Social matters; Verbal communication; Wealth.

FOLKLORE AND FACTS
In medieval times, manipulative beggars would deliberately
rub the irritating *Ranunculus acris* sap on their skin to
make open blistered sores to create sympathy in people
who pass by who might then give them money out of pity
for the beggars' painful-appearing condition.

"Flowers are
like friends;
They bring color
to your world."

–UNKNOWN

AUGUST 2023

NOTES	SUNDAY	MONDAY	TUESDAY
			● 1
	6	7 ◗	8
	13	14	15
	20	21	22
	27	28 SUMMER BANK HOLIDAY (UK-ENG / NIR / WAL)	29

AUGUST 2023

WEDNESDAY	THURSDAY	FRIDAY	SATURDAY
2	3	4	5
9	10	11	12
○ 16	17	18	19
23	◗ 24	25	26
● 30	31		

AZALEA
Sixiang Shu, Thinking of Home Bush

SYMBOLIC MEANINGS
Fragile; Fragile passion; Fragility; Modest; Passion;
Patient; Romance; Take care; Take care of yourself for me;
Temperance; Temporary passion; Womanhood.

FOLKLORE AND FACTS
The honey produced by bees collecting pollen from Azalea
flowers is highly toxic.

July/August

MONDAY (JULY)   31

TUESDAY ●   1

WEDNESDAY   2

THURSDAY   3

FRIDAY   4

SATURDAY   5

SUNDAY   6

August 2023

MONDAY 7

TUESDAY ☽ 8

WEDNESDAY 9

THURSDAY 10

FRIDAY 11

SATURDAY 12

SUNDAY 13

ALCEA ROSEA
Ambition: Ambition of a scholar:
Fecundity: Fruitfulness: Liberality.

August 2023

14

15

16

17

FRIDAY

18

SATURDAY

19

SUNDAY

20

LILIUM LONGIFLORUM

Employment: Gambling: Luck:
Power; Protection.

August 2023

FRIDAY   25

SATURDAY   26

SUNDAY   27

HYACINTHOIDES NON-SCRIPTA
Constancy; Delicacy; Grateful; Gratitude;
Humility; Kindness; Luck;
Solitude; Sorrowful regret; Truth.

CALLISTEPHUS CHINENSIS
Annual Aster, Aster, Aster Mini Rainbow, Callistephus, Rainbow Aster

SYMBOLIC MEANINGS
Afterthought; Beautiful crown; Daintiness; Differences; Elegance; Fidelity; Gained wisdom and good fortune; I will think of it; I will think of thee; I will think of you; Jealousy; Love; Love of variety; Magical; Patience; Symbol of love; Talisman of love; True yet; Variety.

POSSIBLE POWERS
Love.

FOLKLORE AND FACTS
Grow *Callistephus chinensis* to wish for love. • Carry a *Callistephus chinensis* flower to win love.

"Flowers always make people better, happier and more helpful; they are sunshine, food and medicine for the soul."

–LUTHER BURBANK

SEPTEMBER 2023

NOTES	SUNDAY	MONDAY	TUESDAY
	3	4	5
	FATHER'S DAY (AUS / NZ)	LABOR DAY (US) LABOUR DAY (CAN)	
	10	11	12
	GRANDPARENTS' DAY (US)	PATRIOT DAY (US)	
	17	18	19
	24	25	26
	YOM KIPPUR (BEGINS AT SUNDOWN)		

SEPTEMBER 2023

WEDNESDAY	THURSDAY	FRIDAY	SATURDAY
		1	2
◗ 6	7	8	9
13	○ 14	15 ROSH HASHANAH (BEGINS AT SUNDOWN) FIRST DAY OF NATIONAL HISPANIC HERITAGE MONTH	16
20	21	◖ 22	23 FALL EQUINOX
27	28	● 29 SUKKOT (BEGINS AT SUNDOWN)	30

MAGNOLIA ACUMINATA
Blue Magnolia, Cucumber Magnolia, Cucumber Tree

SYMBOLIC MEANINGS
Determination; Dignity.

POSSIBLE POWERS
Endurance.

FOLKLORE AND FACTS
Magnolia acuminata **is the cold-hardiest**
of the Magnolias and one of the largest.

August/September

MONDAY (AUGUST) SUMMER BANK HOLIDAY (UK-ENG / NIR / WAL)   28

TUESDAY (AUGUST)   29

WEDNESDAY (AUGUST) ●   30

THURSDAY (AUGUST)   31

FRIDAY   1

SATURDAY   2

SUNDAY FATHER'S DAY (AUS / NZ)   3

September 2023

MONDAY LABOR DAY (US) / LABOUR DAY (CAN)

4

TUESDAY

5

WEDNESDAY ☽

6

THURSDAY

7

FRIDAY

8

SATURDAY

9

SUNDAY GRANDPARENTS' DAY (US)

10

ATROPA BELLADONNA
Falsehood; Hush; Loneliness;
Silence; Warning.

September 2023

MONDAY PATRIOT DAY (US)

11

TUESDAY

12

WEDNESDAY

13

THURSDAY ○

14

FRIDAY ROSH HASHANAH (BEGINS AT SUNDOWN) /
FIRST DAY OF NATIONAL HISPANIC HERITAGE MONTH

15

SATURDAY

16

SUNDAY

17

DENDROBIUM
Beauty; Friendship; Greed; Joy;
Longevity; Love; Refinement.

September 2023

MONDAY

18

TUESDAY

19

WEDNESDAY

20

THURSDAY

21

FRIDAY   22

SATURDAY FALL EQUINOX   23

SUNDAY YOM KIPPUR (BEGINS AT SUNDOWN)   24

GERBERA
Innocence; Purity;
Purity and strength; Strength.

ANEMONE

SYMBOLIC MEANINGS

Abandonment; Abiding love; Anticipation; Being forsaken;
Estrangement; Every gardener's pride;
Expectation; Fading youth; Healing; Health; Illness;
Love; Refusal; Sickness; Sincere; Sincerity; Staunch love;
Suffering and death; Withered hopes.

POSSIBLE POWERS

Healing; Love; Protection; Protection against sickness.

FOLKLORE AND FACTS

Some legends claim that the same wind that passes over
anemone flowers to open closed petals will be the same
wind to blow the dead petals off of others.

"Love is
flower like;
Friendship is like
a sheltering tree."

–SAMUEL TAYLOR
COLERIDGE

OCTOBER 2023

NOTES	SUNDAY	MONDAY	TUESDAY
		1	2 LABOUR DAY (AUS-ACT / NSW / SA)	3
	8	9 INDIGENOUS PEOPLES' DAY (US) COLUMBUS DAY (US) THANKSGIVING DAY (CAN)	10
	15	16	17
	22	23 LABOUR DAY (NZ)	24
	29	30	31 HALLOWEEN

OCTOBER 2023

WEDNESDAY	THURSDAY	FRIDAY	SATURDAY
4	5 ☽	6	7 SIMCHAT TORAH (BEGINS AT SUNDOWN)
11	12	13 ○	14
18	19	20 ☾	21
25	26	27 ●	28

HELIANTHUS GIGANTEUS
Giant Sunflower, Tall Sunflower

SYMBOLIC MEANINGS
Intellectual greatness; Lofty thoughts;
Misery; Splendid; Splendor; Pure; Pure and
lofty thoughts.

POSSIBLE POWERS
Fertility; Happiness; Health; Sustenance;
Wisdom; Wish magic; Wishes.

September/October

MONDAY (SEPTEMBER)   25

TUESDAY (SEPTEMBER)   26

WEDNESDAY (SEPTEMBER)   27

THURSDAY (SEPTEMBER)   28

FRIDAY (SEPTEMBER) SUKKOT (BEGINS AT SUNDOWN) ●   29

SATURDAY (SEPTEMBER)   30

SUNDAY   1

October 2023

MONDAY LABOUR DAY (AUS-ACT / NSW / SA)

2

TUESDAY

3

WEDNESDAY

4

THURSDAY

5

FRIDAY ☽   6

SATURDAY SIMCHAT TORAH (BEGINS AT SUNDOWN)   7

SUNDAY   8

DURANTA ERECTA
Apathy; Detachment; Indifference;
Tears of departure.

October 2023

MONDAY INDIGENOUS PEOPLES' DAY (US) / COLUMBUS DAY (US) /
THANKSGIVING DAY (CAN) **9**

TUESDAY **10**

WEDNESDAY **11**

THURSDAY **12**

FRIDAY

13

SATURDAY ○

14

SUNDAY

15

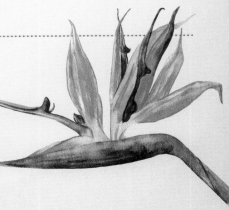

STRELITZIA REGINAE
Faithfulness; Joyfulness; Magnificence;
Romance's surprises; Splendor.

October 2023

MONDAY   16

TUESDAY   17

WEDNESDAY   18

THURSDAY   19

FRIDAY   20

SATURDAY ☽   21

SUNDAY   22

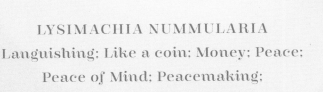

LYSIMACHIA NUMMULARIA
Languishing; Like a coin; Money; Peace;
Peace of Mind; Peacemaking;
Release from strife.

October 2023

MONDAY LABOUR DAY (NZ)

23

TUESDAY

24

WEDNESDAY

25

THURSDAY

26

FRIDAY

27

SATURDAY ●

28

SUNDAY

29

MALUS DOMESTICA
Art; Love; Perpetual concord;
Perpetual peaceful agreement; Poetry;
Temptation; Transformation.

EUSTOMA
**Gentian, Lisianthus, Prairie Gentian, Texas Bluebell,
Tulip Gentian**

SYMBOLIC MEANINGS
Outgoing nature.

POSSIBLE POWERS
Luck; Truth.

"How deeply seated in the human heart is the liking for gardens and gardening."

–ALEXANDER SMITH

NOVEMBER 2023

NOTES	SUNDAY	MONDAY	TUESDAY
	5 ◗	6	7
	DAYLIGHT SAVING TIME ENDS (US / CAN)		ELECTION DAY (US)
	12 ○	13	14
	19 ◖	20	21
	26 ●	27	28

NOVEMBER 2023

WEDNESDAY	THURSDAY	FRIDAY	SATURDAY
1 ALL SAINTS' DAY	2	3	4
8	9	10	11 VETERANS DAY (US)
15	16	17	18
22	23 THANKSGIVING DAY (US)	24 NATIVE AMERICAN HERITAGE DAY (US)	25
29	30		

ALSTROEMERIA
Inca Lily, Lily of the Incas, Parrot Lily, Peruvian Lily,
Peruvian Princess, Petite Alstroemeria, Ulster Mary

SYMBOLIC MEANINGS
Powerful bond.

POSSIBLE POWERS
Fortune; Longevity; Powerful bond with another;
Prosperity; Wealth.

FOLKLORE AND FACTS
Alstroemeria flowers have no fragrance.

October/November

MONDAY (OCTOBER) 30

TUESDAY (OCTOBER) HALLOWEEN 31

WEDNESDAY ALL SAINTS' DAY 1

THURSDAY 2

FRIDAY 3

SATURDAY 4

SUNDAY DAYLIGHT SAVING TIME ENDS (US / CAN) 5

November 2023

MONDAY

6

TUESDAY ELECTION DAY (US)

7

WEDNESDAY

8

THURSDAY

9

FRIDAY

10

SATURDAY VETERANS DAY (US)

11

SUNDAY

12

ZEPHYRANTHES
Healing; Help; Love.

November 2023

MONDAY ○

13

TUESDAY

14

WEDNESDAY

15

THURSDAY

16

FRIDAY

17

SATURDAY

18

SUNDAY

19

ANTHURIUM
Abundance; Adoration; Happiness;
Hospitality; Love; Lusty love;
Romance; Sensuality; Sex; Sexuality.

November 2023

MONDAY ☽

20

TUESDAY

21

WEDNESDAY

22

THURSDAY THANKSGIVING DAY (US)

23

24

SATURDAY

25

SUNDAY

26

PAPAVER ORIENTALE
Dreaminess; Eternal sleep;
Fantastic extravagance;
Imagination; Oblivion.

ILEX AQUIFOLIUM

Aquifolius, Bat's Wings, Christmas Holly, Christ's Thorn,
English Holly, European Holly, Holly Tree, Holm Chaste

SYMBOLIC MEANINGS

Am I forgotten; Courage; Defense; Difficult victory attained;
Domestic happiness; Dreams; Enchantment; Forecast;
Foresight; Good cheer; Good luck; Goodwill; Looking.

POSSIBLE POWERS

Anti-lightning; Attracts and repels energies; Dream magic;
Immortality; Luck; Protection; Protection against harm
in dreams; Protection against witchcraft;
Protection against the Evil Eye.

FOLKLORE AND FACTS

If *Ilex aquifolium* is picked on Christmas Day it will be
very good protection against evil spirits and witches. •
A weather divination that was once frequently taken very
seriously is that if the *Ilex aquifolium* bush had an over-
abundance of berries it was a sign that winter would be
harsh. • The Druids believed that it was an important safety
measure to bring *Ilex aquifolium* into their dwellings in the
winter to give shelter to the elves and fairies who
would house with humans to escape the bitter cold.

"Gardening is
inevitably a process
of constant,
remorseless
change."

–MONTY DON

DECEMBER 2023

NOTES	SUNDAY	MONDAY	TUESDAY
	3	4 ◗	5
	INTERNATIONAL DAY OF PERSONS WITH DISABILITIES		
	10	11 ○	12
	HUMAN RIGHTS DAY		
	17	18 ◖	19
	24	25 ●	26
	CHRISTMAS EVE		BOXING DAY (UK / CAN / AUS / NZ)
	31		KWANZAA
	NEW YEAR'S EVE	CHRISTMAS DAY	

DECEMBER 2023

WEDNESDAY	THURSDAY	FRIDAY	SATURDAY
		1 WORLD AIDS DAY	2
6	7 HANUKKAH (BEGINS AT SUNDOWN)	8	9
13	14	15	16
20	21 WINTER SOLSTICE	22	23
27	28	29	30

JASMINUM GRANDIFLORUM
Anbar, Catalonian Jasmine, Chameli, Jessamin, Moonlight on the Grove, Royal Jasmine, Spanish Jasmine, Yasmin

SYMBOLIC MEANINGS
Sensuality.

POSSIBLE POWERS
Love; Money; Prophetic dreams.

FOLKLORE AND FACTS
Jasminum grandiflorum flowers attract spiritual love. • The fragrance of *Jasminum grandiflorum* flowers help to promote sleep.

November/December

MONDAY (NOVEMBER) ●   27

TUESDAY (NOVEMBER) SUMMER BANK HOLIDAY (UK-SCT)   28

WEDNESDAY (NOVEMBER)   29

THURSDAY (NOVEMBER)   30

FRIDAY WORLD AIDS DAY   1

SATURDAY   2

SUNDAY INTERNATIONAL DAY OF PERSONS WITH DISABILITIES   3

December 2023

MONDAY   4

TUESDAY ☽   5

WEDNESDAY   6

THURSDAY HANUKKAH (BEGINS AT SUNDOWN)   7

FRIDAY   8

SATURDAY   9

SUNDAY HUMAN RIGHTS DAY   10

HELLEBORUS
Anxiety; Calumny; Relief; Relieve my anxiety;
Scandal; Tranquilize my anxiety; Wit.

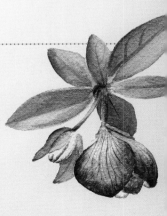

December 2023

11

TUESDAY ○

12

WEDNESDAY

13

THURSDAY

14

FRIDAY

15

SATURDAY

16

SUNDAY

17

EUPHORBIA PULCHERRIMA
Be of good cheer; Good cheer;
Merriment.

December 2023

MONDAY

18

TUESDAY

19

WEDNESDAY

20

THURSDAY WINTER SOLSTICE

21

FRIDAY   22

. . . .

SATURDAY   23

. . . .

SUNDAY CHRISTMAS EVE   24

. . . .

NARCISSUS POETICUS
Egotism; Painful remembrance;
Remembrance; Selfishness;
Self-love; Sorrowful memories.

December 2023

MONDAY CHRISTMAS DAY

25

TUESDAY BOXING DAY (UK / CAN / AUS / NZ) / KWANZAA ●

26

WEDNESDAY

27

THURSDAY

28

FRIDAY   29

SATURDAY   30

SUNDAY NEW YEAR'S EVE   31

POGOSTEMON CABLIN
Abundance; Binding; Breaks hexes;
Energy; Fertility; Friendship; Growth;
Healing; History; Joy; Knowledge.

NOTES

NOTES

NOTES

NOTES

NOTES

NOTES

Inspiring | Educating | Creating | Entertaining

Brimming with creative inspiration, how-to projects, and useful information to enrich your everyday life, quarto.com is a favorite destination for those pursuing their interests and passions.

First published in 2022 by Rock Point,
an imprint of The Quarto Group
142 West 36th Street, 4th Floor
New York, NY 10018, USA
T (212) 779-4972 F (212) 779-6058
www.Quarto.com

Contains content previously published in 2020 as *The Complete Language of Flowers* by Wellfleet Press, an imprint of The Quarto Group, 142 West 36th Street, 4th Floor New York, NY 10018.

Wellfleet titles are also available at discount for retail, wholesale, promotional, and bulk purchase. For details, contact the Special Sales Manager by email at specialsales@quarto.com or by mail at The Quarto Group, Attn: Special Sales Manager, 100 Cummings Center Suite 265D, Beverly, MA 01915 USA.

10 9 8 7 6 5 4 3 2 1

ISBN: 978-1-63106-899-7

Publisher: Rage Kindelsperger
Creative Director: Laura Drew
Managing Editor: Cara Donaldson
Project Editor: Sara Bonacum
Interior Design: Laura Klynstra
Layout Design: Amelia LeBarron

Printed in China

This book provides general information on various widely known and widely accepted images that tend to evoke feelings of strength and confidence. However, it should not be relied upon as recommending or promoting any specific diagnosis or method of treatment for a particular condition, and it is not intended as a substitute for medical advice or for direct diagnosis and treatment of a medical condition by a qualified physician. Readers who have questions about a particular condition, possible treatments for that condition, or possible reactions from the condition or its treatment should consult a physician or other qualified healthcare professional.

All moon phases shown are for the Eastern Time Zone.